Pomegranate Wine

K.L. Raymond

BookLeaf
Publishing

Presentation by *BookLeaf Publishing*

Web: www.bookleafpub.com

E-mail: info@bookleafpub.com

ISBN: 9789357612654

First edition 2022

DEDICATION

For George,

I hope this helps.

ACKNOWLEDGEMENT

Thank you, to every single person who reads this collection. I am eternally grateful.

PREFACE

This poetry collection is based on truth, yet I warn the reader to treat such truth with a grain of salt. Poems are meant to be interpreted, and this interpretation may vary from person to person. Some actions, themes, and situations have been altered, exaggerated, or simplified for poetic effect.

As Ursula K. Le Guin phrased it: "I talk about the gods, I am an atheist. But I am an artist too, and therefore a liar. Distrust everything I say. I am telling the truth."

Heaven's Bowling League

She left me when I was 4,
to sleep forever in a plot of land,
with manicured grass
and wilting flowers.
A selfish act it seemed,
to rest,
while the world weeped above.
Would she not get bored? -
I would think to myself -
Of endless days and endless nights,
peering up at the roof
of her new wooden bed.

As time passed on,
and passed away,
Nan moved again, or at least
she must have.
For no one mentions her in
the ground anymore,
but rather in the sky
instead.
How dare she catch the glass elevator
without me, I think.
I would like to see the
world from up above.

At least I don't need to worry
anymore,
as now, Mum says Nan spends her days
with her parents, sisters,
and friends.
She must have had enough rest,
living underground
for all that time.
But why doesn't she talk to us?
She must not love us
anymore.

I miss her,
so does Mum, but she says
Nan is all around.
The sun is her smiling, reflecting
off her teeth.
Rainbows are just paint,
when she decorates
her new home.
And thunder is the crash
of bowling pins - a loud
one is a strike.

I hope one day to
forgive Nan,
for her selfish, heartless ways.
One day I hope to join her,
be heedless and greedy too.

In ground then sky,
I wish to see her,
look down on the earth,
and become the newest member
of Heaven's Bowling League.

I will be there soon,
I think.
But for now,
it's time for school.

Down the Coast

My father's parents stand on the balcony,
I see them holding hands and grinning,
with chipped teeth, glistening
in the yellow of the summer sun,
I see my mother standing beneath them
on the concrete pavement below,
prepping the barbecue, with a tray of cut
capsicums, potatoes, and carrots at her hip.
My sisters rest in the boat behind me,
sun-baking
while my father guts the bucket of stinky fish,
We are down the coast, we are by the water.
I scream out to my grandparents,
and raise the cold, wet flathead I caught
above my head like a large trophy,
my Nan waves back in approval, my Pop
rubs his belly in a mock display of hunger.
We are youthful,
we are happy.

I am wrong,
I am naive.

I want to go back to the time of this memory,
rip it from my mind and step into it,

like some strange deranged picture frame portal,
and relive the feeling.
It was one of the last times I lived
Without the knowledge of something more,
Something worse than the situation
that could be seen.
I didn't know my Nan was sick, coughing
into a handkerchief behind her back.
I was not aware of my Pop's fading eyesight,
or his fading consciousness as well.
I knew not of my parent's money struggles,
Nor of their inability to express love to
their children as they aged.
I did not think that my sisters would
soon start to bully me, or
would grow uninterested in my company.
Behind the cream-coloured weatherboards
of the beautiful holiday house,
we were broken dolls held together
with glue and propped up by string.

I clutch at the memory in my brain,
like an angry middle-aged man grips
his daily newspaper to swing at the snout
of his disobedient dog.
I wish I could live in the memory, of simple
times
down the coast,
and blissfully catch fish for my smiling family,

for an eternity or more.

What Could Have Been

You probably do not remember this,
but I do.

We talked on Mana's beach,
danced in the alcohol-soaked sand,
and looked into each other's
widened eyes.
We parted ways,
with my heart still racing.
A flight aimed at a city
far from you.

I'm not sure if you ever think of me,
or this single pure moment,
but I do.

I do.

A Trip to the Caves

At the cavern's mouth we stand,
holding hands, only whispers.
A small torch hangs from my throat, on rope.
(A noose?) It flickers.
The cool river cascades through
the cave's jagged limestone teeth.
We wade into the shallow depths. I shake,
he moans. It shimmers.

Way back when, in the ancient chambers,
my parents held the reins.
Look at that! they say - Pose here! they scream.
A pink puppet above red flames.
The cathedral is empty now, that was long ago,
my parents rest in bed; asleep.
But now, I wander the streets - (the cave?) -
alone. Fogged windowpanes.

But as the saying goes, mites go up,
tights come down! - it was time.
I braved the grotto, I swam the seas,
I tasted sweet pomegranate wine.
Little did I know, my mutiny - (his sword?) -
could not render my familiar shackles weak.
In the cavern, I stood, shivering,

whimpering. In search of a broken shrine.

At the cavern's mouth I stand,
tangled hair, violet skin.
In my head, black and white, I see myself
pulled by my parents (on string?)
I shout to endure it, don't act, pay no heed!
Instead, the ghost stares back, and smiles.
It dives, it drowns - unknowing to my kin.

Hero and Leander

No lighthouse in sight.
Rough water, storm clouds, cold wind.
For her, I will drown.

For David

Outside my window, a frog
croaks in the light of the harvest moon.
He beckons me to come out,
to follow.
Drawing back the curtains,
I see his greenish-yellow skin glisten
with briny droplets of sweat.
Putting on my jacket, I head out.
He drives, we chat.
As usual.

When the full moon hid behind the clouds,
the frog did not return.
I left my curtains open permanently,
in hopes of seeing him jump on top
of the rosebush in my garden.
I didn't leave my room,
no croak beckoned me to follow.
I sat, I sat.
Like before.

He reached out later on,
wheezing with his last shallow breath.
His croak was weak.
His skin was grey,

salty perspiration coated every inch.
We exchanged words
of kindness.
Not those of friends, but
those of people who once were.

Although the moon stayed hidden,
waning in the corner of the sky.
I'm glad I got to see it,
stare into the beauty of the wide
rounded moon,
and dance.
He lost his croak too soon.
I owe him.

Midnight's Mistress

The alarm clock that rests upon the bedside table
Provides the only light in the stale room.
The numbers of 11:59 cast a scarlet glow
Over the formless shapes
in the near distance.
First comes the sharp smell of absinthe,
then the thick scent of smoked tobacco;
Midnight staggers through the door.
He wears a pinstripe suit and a bowler hat;
A tie hangs loosely around his neck.

In bed, I squeeze my eyes shut
And raise the volume
Of the music playing through my headphones.
Even so, I can hear him chant my name
Like some Shamanic ritual of death.
Drums echo off the walls;
Stomping feet send vibrations through the floor.
Finally, he takes my head into his hands
And pries my eyelids open with his teeth.
I stare into the void
Of his fang-filled gaping mouth.

Midnight cackles and snaps
His long indigo fingers in my face.

He retreats to the back of my room,
And through the doorway,
His Mistress slinks in wearing nothing but
chains
Around her slender wrists.
She jumps onto my chest and straddles me
Like an old carousel horse,
Digging her sharp knees into my bony ribcage.

For Midnight reclines in the corner,
a bottle of red rum sloshes in his impatient left
hand.
His other jerks back and forth,
down the leg of his pleated black pants.
He watches
As his Mistress unsheathes her poison-tipped
claws.
She drags them across my arms,
my waist,
my thighs,
And laps up the blood with her forked tongue.

With a moan, and a couple thumps, Midnight
finishes;
and tosses a penny to my feet,
He tugs at the iron leash of his Mistress,
who gracefully stands
And plants a kiss on my lips
With the plump violet ones of her own.

Her perfumed breath smells of poppies,
sedating me into a coma-like sleep,
She follows Midnight out of the room.

The alarm clock casts a grey-toned glow
To the empty chamber around me.
It flashes 12:00, but does not change,
Even as the sun comes up in the morning.
I lay bleeding in bed
with a faint taste of alcohol, nicotine, and opium
on my tongue.
No music plays;
Not anymore.

I see Midnight's Mistress hiding behind the
mirror.

The Moth

I have come to realise, that
to be a moth,
would not be an unkind thing.
Brown and speckled,
they are not a spectacle
themself, but rather the humdrum
cousin to the butterfly.
No attention, draws the
simple moth.
They can rest on a wall for hours,
days,
or months,
without experiencing so much as
a glance in their direction.
When has a butterfly ever
lived so discreetly?

Butterflies are not alone in their
dramatic outspoken ways.
A shark can swim close to a beach,
and shut down a whole city's plans
for a summer weekend.
A dog, wandering the streets,
draws crowds of eyes that

wonder if it has a home.
Even cockroaches, which reside on
walls, like the moth,
draw attention at the slightest sight.
Almost as if a spray can is
permanently raised,
ready to destroy the dirty,
brown intruder.

Moths live in the perfect intersection
of dullness.
Too common to draw attention,
and too boring to warrant a reaction.
I envy them.

The Rain

Do not mourn
the death of sunshine,
but rather celebrate
the birth of rain.
It shall wash you clean.

Why Must I Conform To Be Religious?

Let us breathe in the noxious dust,
Of the stale incensed air,
While we pray to a God
Of perfect uncertainty
and unfaltering conviction.
To choke
On his ancient words
Behind spiked iron fences
And beneath rotten exposed beams.
To be whipped
Into starched suits of grey
With blinders covering our milky
Wandering eyes.
To taste the wine, eat the flesh,
Yet have nothing to show for it
But an empty coin purse.
Please listen to the old man,
With fingers in his pants,
But do not do as he does;
Only do as he says.
Be a sheep,
Not a shepherd.
We shall not ask any questions.

Although I would rather
Confess sins to the mountains,
Pledge loyalty to the seas,
And pray faithfully to the skies,
Instead I must remain
Shackled to the rusted altar
Of some dilapidated church.
For it is the way,
Or so I have been told.
Perhaps that is why my necklace
of a golden cross, remains
At the bottom of my sock drawer.

Atheist Pagan

Sometimes, I can feel the energy in the room.
Of the four elements, of the deities, and
Of the miscellaneous objects atop my altar.
Other times, I hear the whisper of the universe.
Of an empty vacuum, of deep space,
And of the pages turning in my textbooks.
I stand at a crossroads,
Between the intersection of complete belief
And total disbelief.
I know the old gods sing to me,
I know the nihilistic void calls out my name.
With my hands pressed firmly to my ears,
and my eyes squeezed tightly shut,
I weep.

A pendulum swings back and forth,
it also remains still.

An Ode to Yellow

My first memories are of sunshine,
of daffodils, golden wattle, carnations,
and of the sweet scent of honey gold mangoes.
I was a summer baby,
my hair was blond, my skin was tanned.
I wore overalls and canary-coloured t-shirts.
Rubber duckies floated in the old bathtub.
Stars adorned my bedroom roof.
On Fridays we ate hot chips and calamari,
coated in chicken salt.
I drank apple juice, but only when watered
down.
Life was too sweet already.

When I went to primary school,
my backpack was decorated with submarines.
We had eggs for breakfast.
I brought bananas for lunch.
In the playground, cockatoos called from the
treetops,
and bees buzzed playfully in the gardens.
We walked down the brick road twice daily.
I drew happy faces on my homework.

It was not until just before my voice dropped,

that the sun turned from bright lemon to deep
dijon.
Vesuvius erupted, coating the world in
the corrupted pigment of Naples.
The mustard gas was always there, I knew that,
it laid dormant in the chambers below.
But suddenly, my sunny rose-coloured glasses
were knocked askew.

You backed me into the corner,
pressed me up against the ochre wallpaper,
and trapped me behind the bars of a piss-stained
cell.
Sulphurous gas leaked from your wide mouth,
while you laughed,
with coffee-stained fangs gnashing
like a voracious shark at the beach.
You were a wicked alchemist, beating my back
with a copper sickle
in hopes of turning my flesh to gold.

You stole the sunshine from me.
You wilted the daffodils, golden wattle, and
carnations.
You ripped the mangoes off their trees,
threw them to the concrete,
and crushed them beneath your leather hooves.

The world became darker then,

as autumn came
and the maidenhair tree lost its leaves.
Hidden in my bedroom,
I began to read stained Parisian books by
candlelight.
I drank whiskey, no ice,
and smoked cigarettes until my teeth
resembled sticks of turmeric.
Under the Dionysian full moon,
I lingered around dark corners, draped in silken
robes,
ripped and coloured like rotten casaba melons.
I wore smeared lipstick,
I smelt of sweat.
A broken crown sat atop my bleached, untoned
hair.

Slowly, summer began to return.
I sat and stared at my reflection in the murky
pond,
scrubbed at my jaundiced skin,
scratched at the amber of my goat-like eyes.
Your shadows stood around me
in a ritualistic circle, with each lily-livered
figure
yelling to each other, and to themselves,
venomous words of a radioactive nature.

Shedding my corn-coloured snake skin,

I slithered away, stood up, and
plucked a daisy from the meadow.
I handed it to a fresh, blond bub
in his mulberry-wood crib, and
rode my chariot into the Tuscan sun.

Sordid Night

The last leaf of autumn dropped down
Onto the cool cobblestones.
Wilted brown, beyond red
It blew around the darkened streets.
Newspapers littered the ground,
The rotten smell of cabbages lingered
In the empty alleyways.
A couple of dogs barked
And yanked at their iron chains.

In front of the hearth,
Ms. Maison's tabby cat
Sat fat
And undisturbed,
Passing a ball of purple yarn between
It's soft plump paws.
Jazz music played quietly in the corner
Of the room.
The fire crackled,
the clock chimed three times.

At the window, beyond velvet curtains,
Figureless shapes peered in
With fiery red eyes.
They scratched at the glass,

Banged at the wooden shutters, and
Licked at the windowsills with blackened
tongues.
Without a glance, the cat stood up,
Circled the rug twice
And collapsed upon a plush pillow.
Its eyes shut
And began to purr.

Outside,
The benches whispered, the trashcans sung,
As if calling for a lover to accompany
Them through the night.
A tramp sat by a lamppost
Slurping up the last remains
Of a sour worm-ridden peach.
A crowd of unwashed, unshaven, unperfumed
things
Huddled in yellow-stained bedsheets
Beneath the bridge.
The stars stuttered, birds choked in dampened
nests.

Ms. Maison's tabby cat shifted closer to the
flame
To warm its chubby pink belly.

Castor and Pollux

To be bonded to another,
As if some divine power
Had decided you were too unbalanced
To be born alone.
As if the world required you to
Have a rivalled partner
To counteract your powerful presence;
Like the night and the day,
Or the killer and the killed.
We do not see singular babies
As being only part-of or incomplete.
But without question, we view
A twin without its other
As only half.
Sometimes I question this bond
Of blood, of nurture.
Do Apollo and Artemis fight?
Do Romulus and Remus get along?
But I figure,
Questioning this connection in the first place
Is evidence of it anyways.
Why care for what does not occur?
The universe gave me an eternal friend.
I am grateful.

Snowglobal Pandemic

Frosted breath fogs up the glass.
However, it snows inside, not out.

I wear a scarf, not for warmth
but because my wooden arms can't bend.

There is nothing to be seen outside,
even if my beady black eyes could see.

Sleds, skies, skates, and snowballs
lay discarded in the ice all around.

After some time, the snow stops;
Sun peers through the glass above.

A boy sneezes,
A woman coughs.

The world is turned upside down,
and the snow begins once again.

It was almost as if life was a perpetual winter,
where we froze, but time didn't.

The 6:48 train there; the 5:23 train home

There is something to be said about
the mindless monotony
of a regular commuter train ride to the city.
The brain-numbing quality,
of passing each station -
day
after day
after day
after day -
Like some Sisyphean torture
of mundanity.
Designed to drain the weak and strong alike,
of any patience
they may possess, and replace it
with the acquiescent conformity
of a person who knows the way,
knows the outcome,
knows the repetition of it all,
yet must bare it.

No joy exists within the
four walls and four doors of the carriages -
not for the regulars at least,

for whom the excitement of travelling
from one place to the next,
has perished.
Stacks of books sit unread,
the newspaper crosswords remain undone,
and laptops reside unused with
emails left unwritten.
Instead, carmine eyes stare out,
not towards the windows,
but towards empty dust-filled spaces.
Large thermoses twitch persistently
in pale, wrinkled hands.
They cannot hear the children laughing.

As time goes on,
the passing shadows draw longer
across the commuters' sallowed skin.
Their faces droop like Daliesque timepieces.
The same timepieces they study,
when counting down the remaining
hours they must endure,
until they have a brief moment of relief,
before returning
the next day.
Again.

Sea Urchin

Perhaps I would be best off living
on the bottom of the ocean,
covered in sharp poisonous spikes,
so that nobody would touch me.

I retch at the thought of intimacy,
heave at the idea of sentiment.
Yet I crave that light addictive feeling,
of being in love. Being with someone.

It's conflicting, to want some but not all,
I feel broken. Dramatic. Lost?
I no longer want expectations or things to fulfil.
However, I crave fatherhood and marriage.

It would be easier to just float and sink,
Allow the seas to choose my course.
But alas, I stay on the land. Suffer.
I shake and wait for the pieces to fall into place.

Escher's Stairs

Endless hallways,
and endless doors,
leads to endless passages,
and endless corridors.

I am lost inside the Labyrinth.
I wish Theseus would lend me his string.
Without knowing what lies ahead,
I am scared. I am suffocating.

Hagstone

The sky is spattered with clouds
of deep burgundy
when peering through the hagstone.

Its ragged edges cut into
the delicate skin of my fingers
as I hold it to my eye —

unblinking,
halted breath,
no noise —

The hole beckons for me to look,
stare into its window,
and weep at its vision.

Three trees point toward
the rising sun,
the middle one set aflame;

as if a god
or higher up power of some kind
had struck it with lightning.

I am not yet of

two and twenty,
and yet I feel even more.

I see glimpses of clocks
set at different times
but unmoving.

I swallow the snake egg.
The tie around my neck
grows even tighter.

www.ingramcontent.com/pod-product-compliance
Lightning Source LLC
LaVergne TN
LVHW010923200726

843509LV00013B/2042